THE
DIVINE
SCHOOL

Donald Wehmeyer

THE DIVINE SCHOOL

Eighty-Eight Chapters

TATE PUBLISHING
AND ENTERPRISES, LLC

Published by Tate Publishing & Enterprises, LLC
127 E. Trade Center Terrace | Mustang, Oklahoma 73064 USA
1.888.361.9473 | www.tatepublishing.com

Tate Publishing is committed to excellence in the publishing industry. The company reflects the philosophy established by the founders, based on Psalm 68:11,
"The Lord gave the word and great was the company of those who published it."

Book design copyright © 2013 by Tate Publishing, LLC. All rights reserved.
Cover design by Rtor Maghuyop
Interior design by Jake Muelle

Published in the United States of America

ISBN: 978-1-62563-457-3
1. Religion / Christian Life / Spiritual Growth
2. Religion / Christian Life / General
13.05.07

DEDICATION

his book is dedicated to
my father and mother
Donald and Helen
my wife
Martha
and our children
Valerie, Kristen, David, Raul, and Constanza
To God be the Glory

PREFACE

Some years ago I was introduced to the sayings (*logoi* or *apogtemas*) of the Desert Fathers, a collection of short notations from third and fourth century Syria and Egypt. In reading these comments I realized the brothers and sisters in the Lord who left them behind had a larger, grander view of the world than I did, even though I lived millennium after them. As I wondered how it was that their universe was so much larger than mine, I noticed a couple of things that seemed individually unimportant but when taken together provoked some new neurons to spark my brain. Whether those sparks produced light or just a scorch mark will be for you to decide.

One thing I noticed about the Sayings of the Desert Fathers is what they did, conveying for us a collection of illustrations of how to think rationally without being restricted to the straight jacket of the syllogism. These authors did not rely on the Greek syllogism as a rhetorical tool. A syllogism is easily illustrated with the equation if A=B and B=C then A=C. Western academia has come to rely almost exclusively on this form of logic. In large part because of our over reliance on this form of logic, we who have a Greco-Roman heritage have lost our capacity to savor the acuity in conundrums, allegories, metaphors, aphorisms, and riddles.

Another detail I appreciated was how the Abbas and Ammas were able to draw useful lessons out of the most mundane event; I think they could do this because they were anticipating that the Word can show up anywhere and at the most unexpected times. This observation showed me in turn how severely compartmentalized our lives are. In today's culture it is only when we enter a classroom that we are students ready to learn; but when we leave the classroom and go to "free time" we allow our compulsions and caprice to have full reign over us. The result of this compartmentalization is the great irony: the classroom has become very narrow and "free time" is when we are most imprisoned by our fallen nature. The narrowness of the classroom is easily seen in that only that which has some potential for empirical results is allowed in. Consequently we have psychologists, sociologists, and philosophers who are technicians just like mechanical engineers, and painters, writers, and musicians are considered entertainers who join us in "free time." This suffocating empiricism, this concrete box in which so many academics have entombed themselves, is the direct result of their anthropology. They can only think of humanity as a species of animal that makes tools for use. This lack of imagination results in complete self-abasement, which is a loathsome thing.

How is it that the Desert Fathers were able to avoid the confining methodology of the syllogism, the sterile distinction between classroom vs. free time, and the misrepresentation of what human kind is? They avoided this trio of pitfalls by appealing in a most matter of fact way to a both simpler and more complex source of authority—an authority that might be identified as Wisdom or Sapience that became incarnate in Jesus the Christ. It is simpler because God is without contradiction or duplicity; God is pure. It is more complex because the Desert Fathers did not reject an important role for rational logic and empiricism in our lives but neither did they ignore the reality of Divine revelation; their world is larger than ours because they hold both the visible and the invisible as being equally real. Their logic might be explained by the proposition: if the Spirit of God is everywhere, then everywhere is where we are most likely to meet the Spirit. The Spirit, the Counselor, makes all of life a classroom and the most boring, lonely, unproductive slavery imaginable is when we are occupied in "free time" which is time away from the Spirit, the Divine Master.

The arrangement of *The Divine School* may seem to be a random pizzicato of chapters. And so it often is, for several reasons. First, in so doing a lesson may appear through an event as much as through words. Second, it is easier to behold in heart and mind a tiny sketch rather than a large, enormously detailed mural. Finally, we usually learn our lessons in an erratic way over a period of time because we are so easily distracted. We begin to pay attention to some

detail of life and then forget it only to have it present itself
to us again on another occasion.

My hope is that you so enjoy your journey through *The Divine School* that you will decide to remain therein.

Blessings,

Donald Wehmeyer

THE
DIVINE
SCHOOL

1.

e left the brickyard.
Leaving the brickyard
he did not know
what he did not know.
He paid little attention
to people, things, or ideas.
He was unable
to choose a graceful response.
He only reacted coarsely.
He had no goal.
He followed only his impulses.
To leave
was an impulse.
He just walked
straight ahead
away.

2.

She had few teeth
walked with a severe limp,
wore ragged clothes
three large warts on her face
and unkempt hair on her head.
She labored to a bench.
The children flocked to her
like pigeons to scattered bread crumbs.
Soon there was laughter.
Watching, he asked to the other with him,
"Why do the children gather round that
ugly old hag?"
The other said,
"The children see what is invisible to you."
"What is invisible to me?"
"That she is a lovely woman."
"Ridiculous. If she was a horse,
the glue factory would reject her."

"The wonder of children is that
they are not yet prejudiced
by the superficial.
That woman holds each child
in high esteem.
She listens to them.
She counsels them.
She celebrates their discoveries with them."
After a moment, the other asked,
"Do you know what makes a person lovely?"
He remained silent.
He did not like
that the other did not share
his opinions.
"What makes a person lovely is
they give their self away in service of others."
He walked away wondering,
What does it mean to give yourself away?

3.

Sometime later, in another place,
a lady washing clothes said,
"I see you are a traveler. I have something for you."
"What could you give me?" he countered.
"A journey is a container. It holds you.
You are a container, you hold a journey."
He said,
"A journey cannot hold anything, and
I am not a container."
She said,
"You have ears but do not hear."
"That's not true, I hear fine."
He walked away wondering,
Why did she tell me that nonsense?

4.

rriving at a crossroads,
he looked left,
right,
straight ahead,
yet stood still.
No decision.
He sat
perplexed.
A man came along
sat near him
and said,
"You will need a guide."
He replied, "Who asked you?"
"You have eyes but cannot see."
"I see fine."
"You cannot see which way to go."
"I can see. I have just not decided."

"You are young. There are no voices in your head."
"Of course not, I am not crazy."
"When you hear voices in your head,
you will need a guide."
"I don't want voices in my head
or any guide telling me what to do.
I want to be free."
The man said,
"To be free from yourself is a most difficult task,
impossible if you are alone."
He walked away.
He did not notice in which direction.

5.

He walked until
he stopped.
A traveler at the stopping point asked,
"The beginning and the end, are they the same?"
"Of course not," he said.
The other
drew a circle on the ground.
"Put a rock on the circle," he said.
He put a rock on the traced line of the circle.
"Is the rock at the beginning or the end of the circle?"
"I can't tell. It seems to be both."
The other
drew a line in the dirt.
"Put a rock somewhere on the line."
He put the rock on the line.
"Is the rock toward the beginning
or toward the end of the line?"
"I can't tell.

It depends from which side you begin."
"The rock is at the point where
the beginning and end are the same.
Look for unity when you see opposites.
He asked,
"How does one learn
to look for unity?"
"You must die to what you see
and live for what cannot be seen."
He thought this is nonsense.
Who can see what cannot be seen?
He walked away
putting
without knowing why
the stone
from the line
in his pocket.

6.

itting on the town hall steps
late at night
he asked out loud,
"What is the purpose of life?"
The town watchman heard and offered,
"It is the very essence of egoism
to want to answer that
question by yourself."
He asked, "Why is it egoism to ask a question?"
"It is not asking the question,
it is the attempt to give your own answer
that is egoism.
You shall never have certainty
starting from yourself."
"But the only thing I am certain of is that I exist."
"Are you the baby in your mother's arms?
Are you the child who played with toys?
Are you the old man lying down to die?"
"I suppose I am all those."
"If you are constantly changing and
you are not in control of those changes,
how certain of yourself can you be?"
Stultified, he demanded,
"Well, how then can I learn the purpose of life?"

"To know the purpose of something
there are two possibilities.
First, a purpose is clear by what the thing does.
The purpose of a tree is to be a tree.
A rock to be a rock.
A river to be a river.
A horse is a horse.
But the purpose of all the trees, rocks, oceans,
and distant planets is different
because
we cannot see the whole universe at once.
We cannot see where it is all going."
"So how can we know the purpose of
everything, including life itself?"
"We need the second possibility."
"What is that?"
"Someone has to tell us."
"What?"
"Someone has to tell us
the purpose of the universe.
There is no other way.
Everything else is presumption."
He wanted to ask more
but the watchman did not stay.

7.

He helped a man
dig turnips
from frozen ground
placing them in a wheelbarrow
to wait their being pushed into town.
He asked,
"Where is the beginning?
What must be done?"
The other said,
"To find the beginning
you must be born again."
He was startled.
He felt mocked.
What the other said
was so impossible.
He walked away
from the turnips
wounded
thinking,
I don't ever want to talk to anyone again.

8.

e walked
until
a river crossed the road.
A dory was tethered by ropes.
Whenever someone arrived to cross,
a man with horse on the other side
would pull the dory across.
He crossed.
Sound in the distance.
Not sound,
music.
Like a moth to light
he went to the music.
He sat.
He listened.
He left his body.

He said,
"That was beautiful.
I was moved."
"Yes," said the musician,
"there is no movement without music."
"I don't know where I went in the music."
"An admirable search, a true quest," said the musician.
"What do you mean?" he asked.
"To search for where one goes
when moved by beauty and music,
that is a noble quest."

9.

He cut timber
with a man who had an easy gait.
The forester asked,
"To what have you given your life?"
He answered,
"I am not a fool to give my life for anything."
The forester continued,
"Everyone gives their life away.
Some to noble things.
Most to ignoble things."
"I do not give my life away."
"Do you know the highest cause
to which to give your life?"
He was silent and unhappy.
He did not like cutting timber with this talk.
"To love God and your neighbors
who carry the image of God
within them."
He walked away
leaving the ax embedded
in the trunk of the tree.

10.

n a town
he went
to a vendor's stall,
covered with a blanket to keep the sun off,
to buy food.
The stall keeper asked,
"How does one keep the first snowflake of winter?
How do you keep a single silver stand of a cobweb?
How do you keep a gentle breeze that passes by?
How do you keep the smell of a baby?
How do you keep the taste of hot chocolate on a cold day?
He said,
"I don't know of any boxes or bags to keep such things.
I don't think they can be kept at all."
The seller laughed
and said,
"I thought you looked like a rabbit
with your foot in a snare.
One must take time to appreciate
then offer frequent thanksgiving
for these gifts.
That is how
to keep
a blessing
a marvel
and a joy."

11.

e left the town with food in his bag.
Then,
without warning,
he felt alert
and knew
he was afraid.
Then,
a short distance away,
looking out
from some shadows
directly at him,
he saw
crouched
a black jaguar.
He felt immobile.
His feet so heavy
he could barely step back
and back
and back.
With distance he felt
more secure.

Then he walked quickly
away.
He found another person.
He told them,
"I saw a black jaguar."
The reply,
"Some would say good fortune was with you."
"You believe me? I said I saw a jaguar."
"I have seen it several times myself."
"But I have never heard of black jaguars here."
"There is much we do not know."
"I could have been killed."
"You met the invisible hand."
He asked,
"How did I meet the invisible hand?"
The other said,
"How do you not?"

12.

At the crossroads, there was a gathering of people.
One man spoke loudly for all to hear.
He listened.
The man spoke of the fall of man.
The man fell completely,
every part of him.
The man fell so hard he was dead.
He did not understand just who had fallen or how.
He thought it was none of his affair and walked on.

13.

He spoke to a woman
picking berries and
putting them in her pinafore.
"Why can't I decide where to go or what to do?"
Putting the next berry away, she said
as she reached for another,
"There are two wolves inside of you.
One is savage
one is peaceful."
That berry put away, she reached for another.
"They fight each other."
"Who wins?"
As soon as the new berry joined the others,
she reach out again
saying,
"The one you encourage the most."
She remained picking.
He walked away wondering,
How do two wolves fit inside me?
How do I encourage them?
And what do wolves have to do
with decisions and direction?

14.

hey were in a boat.
The oarsman rowed.
He asked
the oarsman,
"How do we know the right direction?"
The oarsman said,
"How do the birds know where to fly?
How do the fish know where to swim?
How does the fox know how to care for its cubs?"
He asked,
"Do you think we are like
the birds,
the fish,
and the fox?"
The oarsman
leaning forward,
pushing with his legs,
pulling with his arms
in an easy motion
to powerfully scull the oars
replied,
"All that lives
is guided by the invisible hand."

15.

ater flowed in shallow rivulets.
He crossed on large stones.
A foot got wet.
He came upon
a little group of buildings.
He was surprised
all the doors were open.
He asked,
"What kind of place is this?"
A gentleman replied,
"What kind of place are you looking for?"
He said,
"I don't know.
I was not looking for any place in particular."
"Well then," said the man,
"you have come to the right place."
"But how could that be
if I did not have a place to go?"
"Because you are just where you should be."
"But I didn't know that I should be anyplace."
"Life is full of surprises."
"Should I be here?"

"Do you have a choice?"
"Of course I have a choice!"
"What choice do you have?"
"I can leave. That is a choice."
"It would be if you left."
"I can stay, that is a choice."
"It would be if you stayed.
When do you have a choice,
before or after you have made it?"
He was silent.
He thought,
If I stay, I cannot go, and
if I go, I cannot stay.
He wondered, *Are choices really an illusion?*
"What is an illusion?" he asked.
"An illusion is to believe
in something that does not exist.
The greatest illusion is to believe
facts never change."

16.

On another occasion
while staying there
the gentleman asked him,
"When you look in the mirror,
is the man looking back at you
really there?"
He said,
"Of course not, the man there is only a reflection!"
"But when you leave?"
"Well of course the reflection goes away when I leave."
"So what there was depends on you?"
"Yes."
"Do you see then
how the world depends on you?"
"No I don't see.
The world is not a reflection
in a piece of glass."
"Just like the reflection in the mirror needs you,
so you are most necessary
for the present to be as it is.

You make the world to be more."
"That sounds like vanity."
"Vanity is to think the world is less without you.
That is impossible.
There can be more but never less.
To think the world is more with you,
that is honesty
and honors your Creator.
You change and enrich the world
by your being here."
"I never thought of myself that way."
"Think of everyone you meet that way.
It is the privilege we enjoy when meeting a person."

17.

He stayed.
Days passed.
He thought about the past.
He thought about the future.
He thought about where he was.
He thought about where he was not.
He thought all the whats.
What am I doing here?
What did it all mean?
What is fulfillment?
What is the purpose of life?
He thought about all the whys.
Why was I not born rich?
Why don't people do what I tell them?
Why did I see the jaguar?
Why do I keep the rock in my pocket?
He thought until he thought,
To think more is useless.
The host, seeing him, bowed and asked,
"Are you leaving us?"
"Yes."
"Before you go, I would like to ask you a question.

When you travel, what follows behind you?"
"Nothing follows behind me. I came here alone."
"Have you not been thinking
these many days
of things
that happened
on the way here?"
"Yes."
"So your thoughts followed you here."
"I remember things but do not understand them."
"Events are like gifts presented to you.
Sometimes large, sometimes small, sometimes new,
sometimes like returning friends we have met before."
"Why do you talk of memories
like they are following me?"
"Think of every event as a carrier of a gift.
It is not the event that is important
but what it gives to you.
What it gives to you
follows you.

In fact, I see
prudence, temperance, fortitude, and justice
in pursuit of you."
"How can those words be following me?"
"They are friends which you may allow to join you
or you may push them away."
"How does one meet them?"
"You must know they arrived
where you are
before you."
"So where are they, behind me or in front of me?"
"What does the stone in your pocket tell you?"
He thought for a moment and said,
"Virtues follow behind me and wait before me."
"A wise answer.
Remember
every event can give a gift to you.
Blessings on your journey."

18.

e returned to the road.
A short way past the bend
he came upon a deep stream.
Even before he wondered how to cross,
he saw a coracle.
He paddled across.
The other side seemed quite different.
What was it?
He decided,
it is not this side of the stream that is different
but that I am looking back at where I was,
that is new.
Then he thought,
I will try to remember
what I see depends on
which side of the river I stand.

Later he saw
many people
looking up
at two eagles flying high.
He asked,
"Why do people like to watch the eagles?"
Someone there said,
"We admire the eagles.
The eagles fly toward the sun with their eyes open!
Such a gift to a bird, gives us hope."
"What is your hope?"
"Our hope is for
goodness, truth, and beauty.
To seek them, we must fly toward
the brightest light
with our eyes open."

19.

nce he asked a shepherd
watching over a flock,
"Why is the invisible world important?"
The shepherd said,
"The visible world is shakable,
the invisible is not."
He said, "Is that all?"
The shepherd tested him,
"Are you like a rock
a tree
a bird
or anything else you can see?"
"No."
"Correct, we are not like anything else we can see
except other people."

"I never thought of that.
What does it mean?"
"We are not like anything we can see,
but we are like some other we cannot see."
"Who cares about what we cannot see?"
"Without a relationship
with the unseen other,
our hearts and minds are filled
with selfishness
conceit
loneliness
bewilderment."

20.

On another occasion
he spoke to a man named Mathew.
He said,
"I have heard there is an invisible world,
what does that mean?"
Mathew replied,
"Have you ever seen an infant?"
"Yes."
"All around the baby
people move and talk,
they get blankets,
prepare food
sweep the floor
wash the clothes
dress and undress the child,
yet it is unconscious of all of this.
In the same way the baby is unconscious
of the physical world about it,
many people are unconscious
of the invisible world around them."

21.

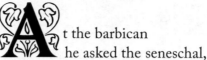At the barbican
he asked the seneschal,
"Why do some men quest,
some travel,
and others are pilgrims?"
"These are the sum of what they can do.
They search, they move, they worship."
"And if they never leave
from where they were born?"
"Some move far away
and never leave their home.
Others never leave their home
and travel far.
To be born is to be born in movement."
"But if they never leave their homes?"
"A quest, a trip, a pilgrimage
is not about moving feet.
They are about what fills your heart."

22.

e observed
a child who would not relent.
The child's face
was red,
his fist
was clenched,
his bawling
loud.
The father
waited, waited, waited.
The child tired.
The tantrum stopped.
Then
the father told a story
to the child.
Afterwards the child kissed
his father
on hand and face
and fell asleep.
He saw patience and a story
are like medicine,
they console and heal.
He remembered,
Any event can be a gift to me.

23.

He arrived in a village
distant from any large city.
On the other side of the street
a young girl served food.
He sat.
When she brought the ewer
for washing hands,
he asked,
"Why do you stay in this place?
Why not go to the city?"
She replied,
"I am waiting for someone to return."
"And what do you do while you wait?"
"I serve everyone who comes to eat
as practice
for serving the one I am waiting for."

24.

The valley was deep.
The cliffs were high.
Evening came early with a chill.
By the brook in the valley
some travelers had made a camp.
He sat among them.
He asked a man with a beard,
"What is power?"
"Power stirs the stillness and quiets the movement."
"Who then is powerful?"
"A person who knows how to join
or walk away from
the stillness
and the movement."
"But a bully is powerful,
he can make you do what you do not want to do."
"In the time of bullies, the hidden hand
is more wonderfully present
than at any other time."
"What does the hidden hand do?"
"It raises our hand
to bless those who torment us."
"What does it mean,
to bless someone who torments us?"
"It means they have no power over us."

25.

e sat and overheard
two men at a table.
One man said
to the other
with a growl,
"I am tired of all this."
The other said, "You sound angry."
With force and indignation,
the first speaker said,
"Of course I am angry,
fate has turned against me.
My horse died.
My crops failed.
My money is gone.
The house roof leaks.
My shoes are broken.
The cow has no milk."
The other was silent for a moment, then said,
"Fate is not against you."
"No? Did you not hear what I said?
If this is not bad fate, what is it?"
The other said,
"It is you.
You have fears and anger inside you
but you imagine them to be outside in the world.

Then you name
what you imagine to be in the world,
fate
and you imagine what you have named
to be against you
trying to destroy you.
You have put yourself in a cage.
You think the world to be controlled by fate
that chews us up
and spits us out.
Remember
within the unchanging rhythms of the world
there remains space for infinite possibilities
because God never stops participating in our lives.
What happens to us
need not happen in vain.
Rather than saying fate is against me,
look for what God is teaching us
through what happens."
The angry man was quiet
as he thought about these many words.
He left the two at the table
and pondered on his way,
Is God teaching us
through what happens?

26.

e smelled the cooking.
He went.
He tasted.
He said, "That is good."
He thought, *To hear music is good.*
He thought, *To eat food is good.*
He thought, *To talk to a friend is good.*
He thought, *To sleep and read and finish a job is good.*
He thought, *With so much good,*
why are so many people unhappy?

27.

e waited until he found
a man in no hurry.
He asked the man,
"Why are there rich and poor?"
The man replied,
"Without intentionality, there is poverty.
With intentionality, there is abundance."
"Intentions are important?"
"Clear intentions are golden.
Confused intentions snarl life."

28.

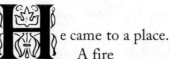e came to a place.
A fire
had burned all the trees and the ground.
Through the blackened soil
came a green sprout.
He noticed the green.
He was attracted to the green.
A small green sprout breaking out of a vast black field.
He thought,
A sprout of courage arrived here before me.
Every event offers a gift.
He left with admiration.

29.

nother day
alone
to think about thinking.
He thought,
To think you are not what you think is presumption.
To think you are not what you do is cowardly.
To think you are not what you say is deceitful.
Asleep, he had a conversation,
"Who is wise?"
"One who knows when to speak and when to be silent."
"How does one learn to be wise?"
"Learn what words are,
learn what silences are.
Then you will have begun."
He awoke ready to learn.

30.

He asked a shoemaker,
"Can you fix my shoes?"
"I can and I will, but may I ask you a question?"
"Yes."
"Where is a cup of tea more stable?
On the back of a goat,
on the kitchen table,
or in the hands of God?"
He thought. Then said,
"It must be in the hands of God. God is all powerful."
The shoemaker smiled and said,
"God has no hands that is why he gave you the table!"
He left with his shoes repaired and a smile.

31.

n the road
a wagon driver invited him saying,
"Why don't you ride along with me?"
He got up on the wagon.
The wagon driver asked,
"What is in your hand?"
"Nothing," he replied."
"Is there no fist?"
"Yes, I have a fist."
"What is in your hand?"
"A fist."
"Is there no caress?"
"Yes, there is a caress in my hand."
"What is in your hand?"
"A fist and a caress."
"Is there no warning?"
"Yes, my hand can warn."
"What is in your hand?"
"A fist, a caress, and a warning."
"Is there no encouragement?"
"Yes, my hand can encourage."
"What is in your hand?"
"A fist, a caress, a warning,
and encouragement."
"Is there no receiving?"

"Yes, my hand can receive."
"What is in your hand?"
"A fist, a caress, a warning, encouragement
and receiving."
"Is there no push?"
"Yes, my hand can push."
"What is in your hand?"
"A fist, a caress, a warning, encouragement,
receiving, and a push."
"Is there no generosity?"
"Yes, my hand can be generous."
"What is in your hand?"
"A fist, a caress, a warning, encouragement,
receiving, a push, and generosity."
"Is there no avarice?"
"Sometimes."
"What is in your hand?"
"A fist, a caress, a warning, encouragement,
receiving, a push, generosity, and avarice."
"Your hand is full.
Take care of what your hand is to give and take."
He took his leave from the driver
and got down from the wagon
with very full hands.

32.

e sat at a table outside a tavern.
He watched.
A boy with trousers too big,
held up with a rope
around his waist and over his shoulder,
ran to greet
a man placidly drinking beer
at the table next to his.
The boy took a moment to settle his breath
and stood as straight as he could
seeming to follow some instructions
he had learned
before addressing the man.
Then he audibly exposed his question.
"How far away is God?"
Looking directly at the lad
the man with the beer said,
"Never more than a single step."
"How high up is God?"
Taking a sip of beer, the man said,
"Look under your feet."
"Under my feet?"
"God is the way.
God is always under your feet."

The boy standing still
moved in six directions at once,
then stood straight again and probed,
"But if I stand in a ditch?"
"God is under your feet."
"If I stand on a rocky mount?
"God is under your feet."
"If I stand at the bottom of a valley?"
"God is under your feet."
"If I stand on a tree branch?"
"God is under your feet.
"If I stand in the deepest canyon in the world?"
"God is under your feet."
The boy's countenance shined
he was at last satisfied.
He pulled at the rope that secured his trousers
and said,
"I hope God does not mind my standing on him,"
then ran off to other waiting marvels.
He thought of the event that evening.
His blessing was to see
the gleam on the face of the boy
who learned God is everywhere.

33.

nce he came upon a monument.
He said to the caretaker,
"What good is a monument?
They are only about things long past."
The caretaker replied,
"A monument is a reminder of brave deeds once done.
A declaration of truth wonderfully told.
A challenge to you to improve the world about you.
An encouragement to those who follow us.
A warning not to neglect what has been won."
He said, "Monuments are reminders to be aware?"
"Quite right," said the caretaker.
He thought,
I had forgotten
every event contains a gift.
Then he said to himself,
Every gift is a monument.

34.

A man
sat at a desk
with many books
on shelves behind him.
He asked the man at the desk,
"Who is powerful?"
"One who desires no power."
"Why am I lonely? "
"Loneliness is living
unaware of the unseen world."

35.

rom the bank of the river he fished.
A visitor he did not know came
and sat beside him.
He asked the visitor, "Who are you?"
The visitor said, "I am a part of you."
"Impossible," he said,
"I have never seen you before."
"Is this not your journey?"
"Yes."
"Am I not a part of your journey?"
"Now you are."
"Now we are.
I am a part of you,
and you are a part of me.
When we meet
we are part of each other."
"True," he said.

They fished together.
That evening
after their meal,
he asked the other,
"How does one celebrate the truth?"
"Search for the source."
"Truth has a source?"
"Like the river, it has a source.
To celebrate truth, search for the source."
"How do we search for the source?"
"How does one search for a buried treasure,
a lost coin,
or a lost lamb?
Pay attention.
Note what is absent.
Seek it out."

36.

ist.
A swamp.
He waded in
up to his knees.
Then to his waist.
He was anxious.
Then after a distance the water was shallower
and he came upon dry ground.
He was relieved.
He felt the heaviness of mud and wetness
on his trouser legs.
He came upon a bifurcation in the track.
Newly confident,
no indecision
he went to the right
ten brisk paces
then abruptly halted
alert.
Why?
He had heard the silence of the forest.
The silence alerted him
to danger.
He looked into the branches above.
No shadows there.
He looked at boulders not far off.

It took a moment to see
a shadow
that moved
slowly, silently, stealthily.
He managed his retreat.
Without turning around, he took seven slow steps back.
On the eighth step he replaced
caution with speed.
He spun.
He fled
on the path to the left.
Later
sitting on a bailey bench
he said,
"Twice I have seen a black jaguar."
Then asked, "Why do I see these animals?"
The companion on the bailey bench asked,
"You were not mauled?"
"I might have been."
"You were not mauled?"
"No, I was not mauled."
"The invisible hand."
"What is the invisible hand?"
"New direction. Refreshed intention. Aha."

37.

he farm hands,
with tools over their shoulders,
were singing on their way down the lane.
He walked alongside them.
Several men shared smiles of welcome.
He asked himself,
how is it that a song
and a smile can change
the way we experience the world?
The gift he knew was to know
songs and smiles
are remarkable things.

38.

nother event came
by a log.
He asked
while sitting on the ground
leaning his back comfortably
against a log,
"Why, when I look at this log
or those bushes over there
or that limb up above,
do I see no straight lines?"
The other sitting handily by said,
"You cannot look with your eyes
to see
a straight line."
Puzzled, he rejoined,
"What else do I have to look with?"
"Straight lines
are not seen with the eyes
but with your memory.
Remember a light
seen from a distance at night.

From whatever angle you approach
the light beam reaches
right to your eye
in a straight line."
"The light comes to my eye in a straight line?"
"And your sight goes out to the light in a straight line."
"Even during the day?"
"Even during the day."
He ran his hand over
the smooth surface of the log.
The bark had gone long ago.
Then spoke,
"So straight lines are in the world but not of it."
"Well said," replied the sitter handily by.
After a few minutes of silence, he asked,
"Are there white jaguars?
"An excellent question." The other smiled.
"A white jaguar is life itself."

39.

hen the log was far behind,
a farmer asked him,
"Can you help cut the hay?"
"Yes," he said.
At midday, they ate together silently.
Then the farmer looking out across the field said,
"The journey is to the beginning."
He said,
"Of course not, a journey is to the end,
to the destination."
The farmer said,
"What is your end?
Where is your destination?"
He said,
"No one can know that."
"Exactly. Since we cannot know the end,
a journey must be to the beginning."
He asked,
"Where is the beginning?
What do we have to do to get there?"
"Those are wise questions," replied the farmer.

"Seek them.
Taste them.
Live them.
Enjoy them.
Where is the beginning?
What must be done?"
They returned to cutting hay.
The next morning the farmer thanked him
for his help.
He departed
with a bit of straw
next to the stone
in his jerkin pocket.
The straw would remind him of the gifts.
Where is the beginning?
What must be done?

40.

e slept in
sty,
pen, and
byre.
Much time passed.
Even so he did not find the beginning,
nor did he know what must be done.
One night he walked
by the light of the moon.
When the new
warm sun rose,
pine needles
offered a comfortable,
scented floor
upon which to lie.
His little pack
became a pillow for his head.
How pleasant this place, he said to himself.
Lying there, he found a question had arrived with him.
Why am I here?

But as he looked above
at the blue sky behind
the limbs
and needles of the swaying trees,
it did not seem to matter.
The pine fragrance
the warm sun
the soft ground
and the birds singing
wrought a drug like result.
He was rendered careless.
Careless
his question
could not hold his attention
and drifted gently to sleep.

41.

e awoke to the sound of
squirrels chattering above.
Two companions returned.
Where is my beginning?
Why am I here?
He tried to ignore them
as pesky midges
which had beaten him many times before.
The evasion failed again.
Then a new
uninvited question
intruded.
"Which way do you ask that question?"
Which way? he wondered.
"Yes, which way?" the intruding thought insisted.
"From right to left or from left to right?"
He held for a moment, then said,
"Why am I here? Or here I am, why?"
"Exactly," said the thought in his head.
"What is the difference?"
"One is disoriented, the other is not."
He mused.
"I came disoriented. I came as, why am I here?
But among these pine trees, here I am."

He sat thinking, *Here I am, why?*
He looked at his rock and the piece of straw.
The beginning and the end.
What must be done?
The end is always a new beginning.
Slowly, he began
to articulate a new treasure
that was birthing in his mind.
Here is the beginning
and here is the end.
Just now here, right now, in this one space
both the beginning and the end.
I am sitting at the beginning and the end.
To travel to the beginning
one has only to finish
what one has begun.
Pleased with his newfound idea,
he did not want to go anywhere.
Time passed.
It was with hunger not music
that the invisible hand
moved him.

42.

An inadvertent step
upon a traitorous stone
injured his ankle with woe some agony.
Sitting,
nursing the ankle,
he lamented.
To be healthy,
to walk easily and briskly is good.
To sit here in pain is bad.
Good and bad
what to seek, what to avoid
are like our left and right feet.
They move us forward
in our thinking.

43.

By the side of the road
an apple seller stood
with a full satchel of apples.
He asked the apple seller,
"How does one choose a path?"
"A wise question.
There is one path that is two paths."
He said,
"I know all paths are north and south,
east and west,
left and right."
"Quite right, the path
I speak of is like that.
It is a path in your control
and not in your control."
"What is in my control and what is not?"
"The choice to resist evil
not to walk down that path
is in your control.
The choice of truth, goodness, and beauty,
to walk down that path
is not in your control."

"Why is one and not the other in my control?"
"Evil comes from within us, it can be controlled.
Truth, goodness, and beauty come from outside of us.
That you cannot control for it is a gift."
"Where does the path that is two paths begin?"
"That which is invisible has no 'where' only when."
"When does the path that is two paths begin?"
"It begins with each step you intend."
"It begins with intention?"
"Only then."
"How do I begin?"
"With two steps."
"Two steps?"
"With obedience and humility."
"Why do we begin with the intentions
of obedience and humility?"
"Obedience honors order
and thereby the creator of order.
Humility confesses
we do not obey very well."
"Why honor order?"
"Because chaos is falsehood."

Mindful of "here I am, why?"
he thought about
obedience and humility.
Then pledged his intention
to resist obediently
and wait with humility.
He had found his new caliber,
resist evil,
wait for truth,
goodness, and
beauty.
The gift of the apple seller,
to know he could censor
the path in his control.

44.

At cock crow
he awoke, he stretched.
A new beginning.
A traveler who had shared the fire
the previous night asked,
"To contain, to show, to release.
Do they have anything in common?"
He said,
"Perhaps to contain and to show
have something in common,
or to show and to release
have something in common,
but to contain and to release
they are opposites."
"See the ember."
The traveler pointed to one with a stick.
"The ember contains heat,
the ember shows the heat,
the ember releases the heat.
In our habit to divide, we forget the unity."

He remembered the stone
in his pocket and said:
"From where I was
I am gone.
Here I am arrived."
"Yes, we are always gone and arrived at the same time."
He thought,
What wonder is this
that to contain and release
and
to leave and arrive,
are the same?

45.

n front of a shop
there was a man
reading a large book.
He asked, "What are you reading?"
"A treasure book" was the reply.
"What is the treasure book named?"
"The book of many books."
"What kind of treasures does it have?"
"Story treasures."
"What kinds of stories?"
"Stories of families,
of wisdom, of war,
of poetry, of slavery,
of heroes, of cowards,
of kings, of illness,
of blessings and of the life to come."
He did not know if a book could be about so many things.
He looked again at the size of the book and said,
"You must be very glad to have such a treasure book."

46.

Lying in a forest glen,
looking with wonder
at the extravagantly star-filled sky,
listening to the crackle, hiss, pop of the fire,
a thought arose;
From mystery I came
and
to mystery I return.
Then
awareness
blended and dissolved
into
slumber.

47.

He passed a windmill
used for grinding flour.
The miller gave him bread.
Later he was joined by a pilgrim.
Sitting under an elm tree they were hungry.
They shared what they had.
He the bread and the other some wine.
Then he was asked,
"Where are you going?"
Remembering the apple seller's gift, he said,
"I am not going, I am waiting for something."
"Waiting for what?"
"I am waiting for something good to find me."
"Are you waiting for something good
or the goodness of something?"
He thought and replied,
"I am waiting for the goodness of something."
Then he added,
"Where does one look for goodness?"
"While you are waiting?
"Yes, while I am waiting, where do I look?

The other said,
"Look where you were,
where you are,
and where you will be."
He liked that answer so he asked,
"How do I look for goodness
while I am waiting?"
"It must be your intention."
The meal was finished.
They walked their separate ways.
He now knew why he had been there.
He had received two gifts,
bread for the body
and intention for his waiting.

48.

The mercer pulled a cart behind him.
Walking alongside, he asked,
"I have heard it said that God
is the same yesterday, today, and tomorrow.
Is God so stiff that he does not change?"
The mercer replied,
"God is continuously active,
this does not change."
"Did not God rest after the creation?"
"God is at rest
because all that is and will be
has been determined."

49.

Jagged rocks and thorns tore his skin.
Cold rain soaked his clothes.
He could see his way only by the flashes of lightening.
The deep mud made lifting his feet an arduous struggle.
He shivered and hunger pained him.
Nearly falling from exhaustion,
he saw a light.
Inside
near a fire
he complained,
"I do not like the journey."
The householder said,
"There is not another one."
"I do not like being bruised and torn by rocks and thorns,
clobbered by hunger and cold,
frightened by fierce animals."
"Are you looking for what you dislike?
"No."
"But that is all you seem to have found
and brought here with you."
"I am not looking for what I like or dislike,
I am looking and waiting for goodness."

"A noble task.
Certainly a better task
than carrying your dislikes everywhere you go."
"I looked and waited for goodness but did not find it."
"Goodness was on the journey with you."
"Impossible. It was miserable out there!"
"You have eyes but do not see.
A thorn that pricks is a good thorn.
A very hard rock is a good rock.
Thick, sticky mud is good mud.
Frigid cold is good cold."
"Is there no evil?"
"Yes there is evil."
"Where?"
"Wherever you stop looking for goodness.
Remember your own words.
You are looking and waiting for goodness.
Be steadfast in your quest."
Rain cascaded off the roof.

50.

e was so tired.
The slope steep.
His pack heavy.
His breath in gasps.
He felt defeat near.
He feared a fall
to his death.
Then, suddenly
unexpectedly,
a man was at his side,
who lifted the pack
from his back,
climbed briskly ahead
and called back in loud voice,
"I will leave your pack at the top."
What is this? he wondered.
With the weight of the pack forgiven,
his confidence was restored.
He easily made it to the top.
He found his pack
and
he found gratefulness.

51.

fternoon
a gathering of anxious people.
A leader yelled
at the top of his voice,
"Ten go to the north,
ten go to the northwest,
ten go to the northeast."
A child was lost.
He joined the search.
At dusk
they heard a cheer.
Superb celebration
broke the gloom.
The child was found safe.
It occurred to him,
life is a search.
The traveler searches for a destination.

The trader searches for goods.
The refugee searches for safety.
The quester searches for honor.
The pilgrim searches for holiness.
The wanderer searches for purpose.
The lost search for where they are.
The poet searches for words.
The musician searches for notes.
He thought,
How much of whom we are
is what we search for.

52.

While on his travels waiting for goodness,
he sat at a table to eat.
A very old man took his order
and brought the food to his table.
"Kind sir," he asked, "why do you wait on me?"
"I do so because it is a privilege to serve whom
my master sends here."
"Who does your master send here?"
"Each person who sits at this table."

53.

A huge shade tree
was waiting there.
He sat
under the waiting tree
with a man braiding
leather strips
into a whip.
He asked the man braiding the whip,
"Is seeking always good?"
The man said, "There is unhealthy seeking."
He asked, "What is unhealthy seeking?"
"Seeking the gift and not the giver."
Then the two were quiet.
When he spoke again, he asked,
"How does one know which way to go?"
"What is your destination?"
Prepared for the question, he answered,
"I should like to go to goodness,
to beauty,
to infinity!"
The man said,
"Look into the eyes of your neighbor
when you speak with them,"
tipped his cap over his eyes
and began to snore.

54.

e crossed to the center of the bridge.
At the center of the bridge
several people leaned on the rail
watching the river flow below.
They were hypnotized by
the silent swirling
the untiring meandering
the unending variations
in the movement
of the water.
He too was captivated
by the effortless creativity
that drifted like a mystery
under the bridge.
He asked aloud,
"Why are there rich and poor?"
A voice replied, "Essences."
"Essences?" he asked.
"Yes, the rich seek the essence, the poor do not."
He asked again,
"Why are there rich and poor?"

"Gratefulness," someone said.
"Gratefulness?"
"The rich are grateful and poor are not."
"Why are there rich and poor?"
"Mimicry."
"Mimicry?"
"Yes, the mimic is poor and the original is rich."
"Why are there rich and poor?"
A voice responded,
"Organization."
"Organization?"
"Yes, the rich work together, the poor do not."
He thought,
Two people each without a coin,
yet one is rich and the other poor.
Two people each with many gold coins,
yet one is rich and the other is poor.

55.

e worked on a farm.
The owners
pleased with his work
kindly asked,
"Are you comfortable here?"
"Yes, for a while."
"Why only for a while?
You are welcome to stay
as long as you like."
"Thank you," he said.
"I will stay until
the invisible hand
jostles me."

56.

he slope was steep.
At the bottom
flat land,
good soil,
a clear brook.
A hamlet was there.
One of the people asked,
"When you walk how do you see?"
He replied,
"With my eyes."
"That is like an animal.
Forget your eyes.
What do you see with your mind?"
"Relationships."
"Yes."
"What do you see with your heart?"
"Admiration."
That individual said,
"You have traveled far and well.
When you walk
use the sight of your mind
and
the insight of your heart."

57.

rom the same hamlet
another asked,
"What do you feel?"
"I feel tired and refreshed
hungry and fed
strong and weak
pain and pleasure."
"Anything else?"
"The wind, the rain, the sun, the cold."
"Anything else?"
"Excitement, boredom, curiosity, anger."
"So you are unaware?"
"Unaware of what?
"Your feet."
"Quite so, I forgot my feet!"
"Appreciate the hardness
the softness
the unevenness
the wetness
the dryness of each step.
This is awareness
not sleep walking.

Without awareness
not only are we not here
but we do not depart nor arrive.
Even when sitting down
be aware
of the rest each toe enjoys."
"I will be aware of each step of my feet," he said.
"So you are unaware?"
"Of what?"
"Of your breath.
Each breath you take inhales peace or discord."
"I will be aware that I inhale either peace or discord."
"So you are unaware?"
"Of what?"
"Of what you hear?
Everything you hear brings truth or falsehood."
He said,
"Our bodies can tell us many things by careful
awareness of our steps, our breath, and our hearing."
The person nodded satisfied.
That affirmation was a
refreshing encouragement for him,
a gift more precious than gold.

58.

he cook Lydia was always a happy woman
but happier still when preparing a meal for others.
He asked her,
"What is emptiness?"
She replied
talking with a wooden spoon in her hand,
"Your life is like an invisible room."
"What is in the room?"
"There are many people and things in your room."
"Is the room big or small?"
"The size of the room changes frequently.
Emptiness is sometimes so big it cannot be ignored
and sometimes it is so small it can be overlooked."
"Is the room spacious or tightly packed with things?"
"One person has a large room
filled with just a few things."
"Another person has a small room
filled with many, many things."
"Why does the room change size?"
"The height and width and length of the room
grows each time you
learn
enjoy
love
desire.

The height and width and length of the room
diminishes each time you mien
avarice
lust
anger
sloth."
"What is happy emptiness?"
"Faith that your room will be filled
with beauty, truth, and goodness."
"What is sad emptiness?"
"A room
without intention or gratitude,
without obedience or humility,
without beginning or end."

59.

The cartwright worked.
He swept the floor.
He asked the cartwright,
"What is the measure of a person?"
The other said,
"Their labor for a better life,
their acceptance of standards,
their knowledge of quality,
their refusal of low desires.
He thought and asked,
"What is prison, and what is escape?"
"Prison is the downward
spiral of life.
Escape is the upward
soar of life."
"Is escape possible?"
"Only when we say,
I am the maker of my own bed
and in it I now lie."
"How are these words of escape?"

"They are words of escape
because
they are a confession of responsibility.
Each one is responsible for how
they respond to life.
I make my own bed and lie on it.
If I do not like my bed,
I must get out of that bed and change it."
Crossing a field that afternoon he thought,
Only the responsible soar upward.

60.

He stopped by a
spring
to drink.
A young woman wearing a dirndl
was there filling
demijohns in woven wicker
set upon a cart
pulled by a pony.
He drank cool water and sat to watch.
She asked him as she worked,
"When you drink water,
what water do you drink?"
He did not know what to say.
"The water at hand" was all he could reply.
"The water you drink
was created
from mystery.
It has been on earth
since
long before mankind.
It sustains all life.
It washes every creature.

It provides a home for the fish.
It is soft in the mist
yet cuts canyons through the mountains.
When you drink water,
what water do you drink?"
"I drink a gift of the mystery of life
past,
present, and
future."
"Yes," she said.
"Each drink of water
is an experience
of mystery and blessing."
He thought the water there
tasted sweeter
than any other he had ever known.

61.

The painter sat before his easel.
He painted a mother and daughter
selling flowers from their dray.
He asked the painter,
"Who are people?"
"They are pieces of a mosaic."
"What mosaic?"
"The mosaic of life.
Each person completes
the mosaic
that is life today."
"Who are happy people?"
"Those who create."
"Why?"
"They are most like the Creator."
"What was the first creation?"
"A story shared."
"Happy people are they who
create and share stories?"
"Yes, you are correct."
"Why do stories make people happy?
"Stories carry reminders of what they have forgotten
and anticipate what they have yet to learn."

"How do we know our place in the mosaic?"
"Listen to the stories of others
when they will tell you.
Tell your story to God
when you are alone.
Tell your story to others
when they will listen.
This is the way to learn
your place in the mosaic."
He left pondering the thought,
To learn
who are people,
I listen to stories
and
tell my story.

62.

nce he was looking intently
at a twig on the ground;
a thought budded in his mind.
What if the tips of the twig
were each a reminder of his travels?
The thought bloomed.
Each tip represents
a different part of the story.
He began to name the tips.
Giving, receiving
helping, listening
learning, silence
preparation, disappointment.
Looking intently
at the twig on the ground
he was certain there was more to remember
but the twig was small
and every tip had been named.

63.

He climbed
past the trees.
He found a pleasing knoll.
There he sat in the wind.
He looked around and thought,
I sit under the bowl of heaven.
He observed,
*Under the bowl of heaven
there is no place to hide or to be lost.*
The peacefulness was soporific.
Rain woke him later.
He smiled.
The invisible hand was now sprinkling him awake.

64.

carpenter was making a table
in the shade of a tree.
He asked the carpenter,
"What does it mean
the world and we are mirrors?"
"The world and we are mirrors
because we can reflect each other.
The world of physical things
sticks
rocks
and decaying leaves
is totally indifferent to us.
They do not regard us with favor or displeasure.
When we reflect this physical world,
we too are indifferent to existence,
we become like
sticks
rocks
and decaying leaves.
When the physical world reflects us,
the sticks
rocks
and decaying leaves
are not indifferent but have stories to tell,
and the world becomes a wonderful place to live."

65.

man with tattered clothes commented,
"The abundant life is full of searching."
He queried,
"How can one be full searching?
We search for what is lost
not for what we have."
"Searching refers to fulfilling an absence.
An awful absence produces an awful search."
"But should we not wait for goodness?"
he asked.
An awful search is the most sacred way
to wait
attentively
intelligently
respectfully."

66.

county fair brought many people together.
One youthful man
leading four small pigs
exploring with their snouts
pulling in divergent directions
asked him,
"Are
stalemate, conundrum, exhausting
the same as
complete, resolution, peaceful?"
"Such a question!" he exclaimed.
"Can you ask that again?"
"Is stalemate the same as complete?
Is conundrum the same as resolution?
Is exhausting the same as peaceful?"
He deliberated
brow furrowed.
His reply,
"They are not just different,
they are perfect contraries!"
The little pigs were now quiet underfoot,
their minder asked,
"Is there unity among them?"

"How can there be unity among contraries?"
"They are all responses.
You and your journey are one;
there is completeness, resolution, and peace.
You and your journey are antagonistic;
there is stalemate, conundrum, and exhaustion.
The contraries find unity in you."
He thought as the man walked on,
I hope he gets a good trade for the pigs.

67.

t the fair, a baker said,
even while he smacked and kneaded,
kneaded and smacked
the dough on a board by the oven,
"People who say, 'I do not like this journey,'
believe in fantasy."
He watched the baker work the dough,
then asked, "Why?"
"There is no other place to be
than where we are."
"But what is the harm
of imaging you could be someplace else?
It could ease the pain."
"Fantasy is neither healing nor creative."
"Why?"
"Healing and creativity transform
what is into what can be.
Fantasy destroys the present,
forgets the past,
and ignores tomorrow."
"How are things transformed?"
"We transform the things around us
with apology and humility, never dislike."

"What do you mean?"
"A farmer prepares the field,
a tree is standing there.
The tree is cut down
with apology not dislike.
The ground is hard
it must be broken to take a seed
with apology not dislike.
The wind is cold.
The door is shut.
The wind is kept out
with apology not dislike.
No task is well approached with animosity.
No task is not well approached with gentleness."
The gift he received,
the only place to be is where you are.

68.

A dense calico pattern of alpine flowers
joyfully covered the meadow in total riot.
His fingers linked together
made a pleasing cradle
to put
behind his head
as he lay back
amidst the flowers
on the soft carpet of grass.
Above hung vast white clouds
slowing moving
before the deep blue firmament.
I should build a house here,
he thought.
No more leaving.
Just here.
He stayed
and stayed
and stayed.
Then a thought
discovered him,
flouted his reproof
and insisted on his declaring,
"I am bored."

He asked himself,
Is there no perfect place
where one is not bored?
Then suddenly
astonishingly
the boredom vanished.
A new
exciting idea
came up.
He apprehended
the perfect place
was not about geography.
The perfect place
was
an attitude
not a location.
The perfect place
was
the correct attitude
for seeing the world.

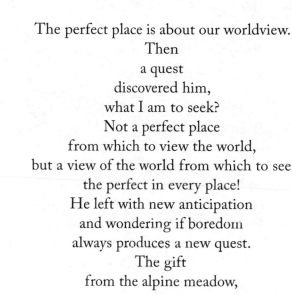

The perfect place is about our worldview.
Then
a quest
discovered him,
what I am to seek?
Not a perfect place
from which to view the world,
but a view of the world from which to see
the perfect in every place!
He left with new anticipation
and wondering if boredom
always produces a new quest.
The gift
from the alpine meadow,
a quest
to see
the perfect in every place.

69.

uring the night
rain, thunder and lightning.
In the morning light
a swollen stream and a plaintiff cry.
He went to the cry and saw
a thin man struggling to hold on to
a fat woman being pulled away by the maniacal stream.
He stood before the danger.
His feet did not move but his heart raced very fast.
He tried to think but his head was stupid.
Then a heavy blow to his back compelled him on
as a man raced ahead shouting, "Come on, let's help."
The redeemed were wrestled to the grassy bank
exhausted.
The thin man looked at him with a scowl
before which he stood
mute.
The savior said,
while wringing dry his shirt,
"Don't worry my son, now you have seen how it is done."

Walking away
he could not leave the scowl
or the words
behind.
He wondered,
How does a brave man not judge me a failure?
How does courage nourish the weak to be strong?
How does fear render a strong man weak?
Many miles later he thought,
To emulate that brave man,
to slap someone on the back and say,
'Come on, let's help'
I will have to be a new person.
In the distant field he saw goats eating grass
and he sighed alas.

70.

hile the snow was very deep,
he stayed at a farm
to help with the animals.
The farmer could not see well.
He asked the farmer
who could not see well,
"When I am afraid, what shall I do?"
"Fear comes from ignorance or prudence,"
said the farmer.
"How does fear come from two places?"
"A lion charges to eat you.
High intensity ignorance is unhelpful,
it is paralyzing. You will be a ration for the lion.
High intensity prudence is most helpful,
it propels you up a tree quickly!
But do not dislike the lion;
it has no control over such impulses.
It could not have acted otherwise.
So when fear comes,
let it be born from prudence
not ignorance,
and climb down from the tree
only when the lion is gone."

71.

e entered the orchard.
The caretaker was up high on a ladder.
He asked,
"Will you hear my supplication?"
The caretaker said,
"I listen to the tress, I will listen to you."
"Do you have advice for the trees?"
"I have companionship for the trees."
He asked,
"Why are people afraid to change?"
Still on the ladder the caretaker said,
"To change is a sacred act.
To change is act like God."
"Why is changing to act like God?"
"God adds, creator.
God heals, redeemer.
God supports, sustainer.
To change touches
three things of God."
"Is it not said that God does not change?"
"God's intention does not change.
Creator, redeemer, sustainer
describe the one eternal intention of God."

72.

ho is a graceful person?"
"A graceful person lives gently."
"How does one live gently?"
"By seeing beauty in all things."
"When will I see beauty in all things?"
"At the time you forgive the ugly."
"How does one forgive the ugly?"
"Gratefully accept
its contribution to your life."

73.

A man had a dog.
The dog did tricks.
The people laughed and gave him a coin or two.
He asked the man
with the clever dog,
"How can you live in something you cannot see?
How do you know it exists?"
The man with the dog asked him,
"Can you see China just now?"
"No."
"Do you agree it does exist?"
"Of course."
"Do my memories exist?"
"Yes."
"Yet you cannot see them.
Do you see your own words?"
"No."
"Now you know
you do not have to see something
for it to exist."

He pressed on asking the man with the dog,
"But to live in the invisible world
do you eat invisible bread
walk on invisible ground
sleep in an invisible bed
talk to invisible people?"
"It is not possible to live only in the invisible
world because you have a visible body.
What can be learned
is to remain aware
and respectful
that all that is visible
emerges from the invisible."

74.

He had been waiting to ask
now he asked the gardener,
"How is it that soil and water
produce a beautiful flower?"
The gardener said,
"The soil and water do not produce a flower."
"What then?"
"A beautiful flower bloomed
and produced a seed.
The seed fell from above the earth
down to the ground
died, and was reborn.
Amidst the soil and water
it grew and beautifully bloomed.
Every flower is a sign
of the intervention
from above the earth."
He thought,
The gift is to know,
flowers are from above.

75.

he other asked,
"Why did you leave the brickyard?
Was it your desire?"
"I had no desire."
"Was it your plan?"
"I had no plan.
"What was it?"
"I only had an urge to go."
"To go where?"
"I wanted to go
somewhere."
"The urge to go
is a thirst for freedom."
"What thirst?"
"The thirst that must be satisfied with care.
There are many mephitic wells.
Wells that do not quench the thirst
but make it ever greater."
"What freedom?"
"Freedom from separation,
freedom for unity."

"What separation?"
"Once we see we are unlike
everything else in the world
we feel separated,
trapped in our aloneness.
To be free of aloneness
only union with the universe will serve."
"So how do I
quench the thirst and
find freedom for unity?
"Your steps must lead you to God."
"To God?
But where does one go
to walk to God?"
"To walk toward God
you walk toward understanding."
"But I don't understand anything!"
"Exactly true. A good beginning."

76.

here was a man with a net.
He cast it wide and true into the pool.
No fish were retrieved.
He cast the net again and again
neither harried nor dispirited he worked.
He stood by the fisherman's side and asked,
"How do you become someone new?"
The fisherman said,
"Do you want to know how, or when, or where?"
"All of it, I want to be someone new."
"Then open your eyes in the morning,
walk attentively through all doors,
listen to a grandfather's story,
enjoy the weight of the water you carry for another,
cut away the brambles,
teach a child to make a kite that flies
and a pinwheel that twirls,
and never, never forget
to build a bridge across a stream."
"If I do these things will I be a new person?" he asked.
The fisherman looked into his eyes and said,
"You are new when you charge
forward to live these things."

eneath a shade tree
A family
was shucking corn.
He sat to help
and asked,
"How can you hold
something invisible?"
The eldest woman said,
"The desire to hold something invisible
and holding an object in hand
is the same thing."
Twice he pulled at the green husk,
then said,
"That makes no sense.
How can the desire for something
and holding something in your hand
be the same thing?"
A young man, her grandson, smiled and said,
"It is not the thing you desire
or the thing in your hand
that is the same.
It is the holding them that is the same."
He looked at the grandson and replied,
"Something invisible and something visible
cannot be held the same way!"

"You are right!" They all said together
delighted.
"I am confused," he said.
A girl not yet big with no shoes
and hazel eyes said,
as she cleared the last filaments from her ear of corn,
"We hold invisible things in our desire for them,
we hold visible things in our hand."
"So why do you say they are the same?"
The girl's mother asked,
"Have you ever watched an infant hold a toy?"
"Yes."
"What happens?"
"They throw their hands in the air
and the toy flies away."
"Exactly."
No one said anything more.
He was befuddled.
He said,
"I am still confused."
The mother,
looked at him like a teacher intent on her task.

She gripped
an ear of corn in her hand,
and said,
"To hold something in your hand
you have to know it is there
you have to pay attention
so not to lose it unaware.
Now think about a desire.
You have to know it is there.
You have to pay attention,
be aware
or it flies away.
To hold an invisible thing in your desire
and to hold a visible thing in your hand,
is the same
because they both require
your careful
attention
and awareness,
or they fly away."
They generously gave him corn
to take with him on his way.

78.

"Who is a disciple? "
"One who makes the invisible visible."
"What is faith?"
"The enjoyment of unseen company."

79.

e was asked,
by a boy leading a donkey
loaded with sundry baskets,
"How many of you are here?"
"There is only one of me."
"If you are one, then you are three."
"No, I am alone."
"You are
your body
your mind
your will,
three yet one.
The body feels pain and pleasure.
The mind receives the truth.
The will searches for goodness."
He was enchanted and said,
"You are right. I am three in one."

80.

While sitting in a circle
around the fire,
he heard a robust conversation.
He realized
the people spoke of wonderful things
sleek horses,
drinking and dancing,
catching rats,
sharp knives,
hoodwinking the bailiff,
yet he felt distant.
As he wondered,
Why do I feel distant?
he was surprised
to find
he had the answer.
He smiled.
He knew the invisible hand
had touched him.
He said to himself,
I seek not the wonderful
but the maker of the wonderful.

81.

They stood watching the activities.
He asked another person
who shared the post he leaned upon,
"Who are happy people?"
The other said,
"Happy people are those who create."
"Why?"
"They are most like the Creator."
"What was the first creation?"
"A story shared."
"Why was the story first?"
"It was story
that created
the immensity of the universe."

82.

e sat next to a man
to watch
a vine become a basket.
The man sat among many vines.
He stripped them of their leaves.
He wove the vines with a whistler's tune
and lo they became
strong baskets.
He asked the weaver,
"How do you become someone new?"
The weaver replied,
"What do you put down and what do you pick up?"
He said to the weaver,
"I put down what I don't need and
pick up what I do need."

The weaver laughed a very hearty laugh,
"If that were so you would be who you are to be."
He remonstrated with vigor;
"I want to be different, I want to be
courageous and not be afraid."
The weaver said with a quiet voice,
"Learn from the vines:
courage like a vine can be found;
fear like a vine can be controlled."
"Where is the vine I need to find?"
The man stood and stacked his baskets on a cart
ready to start away he said,
"Good cheer my friend, the vine is not lost."

83.

e carried rocks
for an ashlar mason
who rarely spoke.
"I have searched and waited
so long
for goodness,
yet I am defeated."
The mason rested his hammer
on his lap
and said,
"When you extend your hand
to search for goodness,
or wait for goodness to arrive,
you have already reached too far
and waited too long
for the goodness you seek has
been given and has already arrived."
He was glad to hear
the words just said,
"The goodness has been given?

It has arrived?"
The mason with his arm
still at rest
smiled yes.
He asked, "Where?"
The ashlar mason said,
"Goodness is always with you."
"But where, I don't see it, how
can I know goodness is with me?"
"What does a lost child do?"
"The child cries out for its mother."
"Call out for goodness and you will find it near."
He said,
"Oh, dear goodness, find me!"

84.

e scrambled up a slope
so steep
he could not see
over the top.
Reaching the crest,
his mouth fell open.
He saw
a vast ocean.
Even from the height of the hill,
he saw no other side.
Before the immense sight,
he saw
the shore
was the beginning
and the end.
He saw
white billowing sails looked like wings
and the wind moved the ships
as it blows leaves across the ground.
He went
down to the quay.

Large bales, boxes
casks and chests
were being hoisted aboard.
"What place is this?" he asked.
"Are you looking for a place?"
He thought, *I am looking for goodness.*
He asked, "Is this a good place?"
The man said, "Yes if you brought a good heart."
He slept under a skiff.
Heavy rain fell during the night.
He stayed dry and warm.
Morning brought
dazzling sunlight reflected off
the shimmering surface
of the sea.
Blinded by the brilliance,
he felt
a hand upon his shoulder
and heard
a strong voice ask,
"Are you a sailor?"

He said,
"I am not a sailor. I don't know what to do!"
"Only an honest heart would say that.
Would you like to be a sailor?"
"Is the ship safe?"
"How safe are the towns and mountains?
"Why do people go aboard?"
"They have walked enough
by their own two feet.
Now they want the wind to
carry them."
"But I am afraid."
"In the ship we are together."
"Who are the crew?"
"You have met many on your way.
You know Mathew,
the shoemaker,
the hay farmer,
the old man waiting on tables,
the miller, and many more."

"I did not know
they were crew members of your ship!
But I do not want be a burden."
"Since the beginning of time, the wind blows
around the globe.
It does not stop.
If blowing a large ship across the water
is not a weight upon the wind,
how will your presence be a burden?"
"But the ocean is so vast, so deep."
"There is far more water than land in the world."
"But I have so many questions and doubts."
"These are welcome too."
Then the hand
and brilliance were gone.
When he could see
no one was near.

85.

Not far away
a large crowd.
Someone called out,
"The food is ready. Please sit down at the tables."
He was hungry.
He sat.
Baskets passed
each guest took
grilled fish, bread, milk, and honey.
They drank, hot tea that warmed their gullets.
At his table there was a man called Captain
who had authority unlike anyone he had ever met.
He asked, "Captain, what is your ship?"
"It is a school."
"Who can go on board?"
"Those who intend to leave the shore behind."
"What does it teach?"
"To be fishers of men."
"What will happen if I go?"
"Then one journey will have ended
and another will begin."

"What must I do to go aboard?"
"All that is necessary was done long ago."
"I have been approved?"
"You were approved
before you left the brickyard."
"How did you know I was in the brickyard?"
"Do you believe the impulse to leave there
was your own?"
"Why didn't I know?
"That is a great mystery."
"But I could have come here much sooner."
"Give thanks you are here now.
Time is never lost."

86.

he ship was a new world.
He had to learn a new way of walking.
Many times he slipped
landing hard
on his backside.
The sudden jolt made him laugh.
He loved that the crew
laughed with him.
He was attentive
knew deep gratitude
and found the pleasure of fellowship,
honor
and service.
He esteemed obedience
beauty
and goodness.
He cherished humility
learning
and teaching.

He discovered generosity
courage
and hospitality.
He loved forgiveness.
They were all there on the ship.
He knew them all by name.
They were his companions and friends.
With desire and affection,
he held each one
in his heart.

87.

e awoke.
He awoke as never before.
He looked for a word
to describe the newness
the differentness.
He struggled
until he found
the perfect word.
It was joy.
He had awoken
joyful.
It was so new.
What had vouchsafed joy to him?
So many questions
flooded his mind.
Questions not burdensome
because
they did not have to be answered
just now.

Joy
he found
was new knowledge.
Knowledge
that life
was complete
and fulfilled
journeying
with the wind,
the captain, and
the invisible hand.

88.

o he said to us
who read his story,
"It is a joyful blessing
to come upon
the threshold of home
walking, asking, rowing, hearing,
limping, shivering, seeing
and climbing
through the divine school."